BELLA LAMM

22 Hours
A JOURNEY
THROUGH
ETERNITY

Glimpses of Things Unseen

TRILOGY

PROFESSIONAL PUBLISHING MEETS POWERFUL PROMOTION

A wholly owned subsidary of TBN

Trilogy Christian Publishers

A Wholly Owned Subsidiary of Trinity Broadcasting Network

2442 Michelle Drive

Tustin, CA 92780

For information, address Trilogy Christian Publishing

Rights Department, 2442 Michelle Drive, Tustin, Ca 92780.

Trilogy Christian Publishing/ TBN and colophon are trademarks of Trinity Broadcasting Network.

For information about special discounts for bulk purchases, please contact Trilogy Christian Publishing.

Manufactured in the United States of America.

10 9 8 7 6 5 4 3 2 1

Library of Congress Cataloging-in-Publication Data is available.

ISBN 979-8-88738-095-7

ISBN 979-8-88738-096-4 (ebook)

"While we do not look at the things which are seen, but at the things which are not seen. For the things which are seen are temporary, but the things which are not seen are eternal."

2 Corinthians 4:18 (NKJV)

Table of Contents

Acknowledgments

I want to give thanks and praise to my Lord and Savior, Jesus Christ. Without Him I can do nothing, and with Him nothing is impossible. He has given me insight to His Kingdom and His heart, and I am eternally grateful to know my loving Lord.

I also want to thank the beautiful people that God has placed in my life who have come alongside me as I continue in the vision God has placed in my heart.

Neolla Hanekom, thank you for your graceful leadership in overseeing the details of this project and for serving with me in the homeless ministry since 2018. You and your husband Neil are true friends and have been amazing supporters in endless ways throughout this journey.

Ashley Hale, thank you for being so dedicated in creating beautiful and Holy Spirit inspired art and setting up ways to reach so many people with this message through social media.

Barbara Gibson, thank you for offering your insight and guidance in the writing process, and for using your God-given talent to make our many projects that seemed insurmountable become fun and achievable.

Amber Peña, thank you for bringing encouragement and for using your creative writing gift to convey my story in a way that is inspiring and relevant, as we relied on the Holy Spirit every step of the way.

Debbie Nemcovich, thank you for being so wonderful at seeing how things fit together and for offering your gifted editing skills.

Mary Anne Arnel, thank you for serving alongside me in my ministry and your heart to help all of us who have an inspired vision to further the Kingdom of God in such a fun and brilliant way.

Myrna Paprocky, I am grateful for your friendship and service to the homeless and thank you for using your editing skills to help perfect the writing in the process.

I am honored to call each of you my friends and appreciate how God has used each one to bring this vision into reality. He is worthy and to Him be all the glory, honor, and praise!

Foreword

It is such a pleasure for me to speak of this wonderful servant of the Lord, Bella Lamm, who has been a faithful member of my church congregation in Jacksonville, Florida since 1986. Bella has served in and been an asset to New Life Christian Fellowship in more ways than I can count. Her gift of hospitality that she so generously shares has blessed my family as well as many of my congregants. It is a true honor for me to be her pastor.

This quiet and unassuming lady makes a great impact for the Kingdom of God everywhere she goes. She is a servant to the Lord who ministers to the homeless on the streets of my city. We have seen hundreds of lives transformed by her acts of kindness and her willingness to share the gospel with those who are most needy.

This book is her story, but it is also a great inspiration for all Christians to follow. The most important lesson to be learned from Bella Lamm is that being filled with the love of Jesus demands action on the part of the believer. How many times have I seen people worship the Lord but never follow through by walking in His nature? Bella has excelled in representing Christ to this world in a way that draws people to Him and brings them to repentance. Her life shines brightly in the midst of great darkness!

Please consider this all-inspiring life of a single individual and see the lessons we all can learn from expressing the beauty of Jesus to those who are in great need. I am confident that Bella's life will continue to make a great impact on generations to come because of her unwavering commitment to God! I pray that her spiritual heart will be transferred into every believer who reads this book.

Bishop Paul D. Zink

Founder of New Life Christian Fellowship and Providence School

Jacksonville, FL

"Prologue"

BY NEOLLA HANEKOM

The saying, "God uses ordinary people to do extraordinary things" has been burning in my heart lately. I cannot think of a better example of this than Bella Lamm, whom I have the privilege to call friend and sister in Christ.

Since I met Bella in 2017, she has constantly amazed me with her humility, compassion, tenderness, love, care, affection, and selflessness. Perhaps the most outstanding quality Bella has is her unbroken commitment to God! Out of the multitude of people I know in this world—and many of them wonderful people—she is the most committed person I have ever met (and that is not an overstatement).

Bella also has a gift of hospitality, which has been a blessing to so many whom she has touched with her life. I would actually call it an anointing, because of the effect it has on people that is beyond the physical realm. She loves to host people in her home, feed them, and send them out with a big smile on their faces and joy in their hearts. The value she puts on fellowship and the sacrifices she makes to honor people in her life is a true example of godliness, which, according to 1 Timothy 4:8 (NKJV) is "profitable for all things, having promise of the life that now is and of that which is to come."

I have been able to learn so much from spending time and serving alongside Bella in the outreach ministry to the homeless in Jacksonville, Florida, since 2018. We have had many incredible moments of fellowship, worship, prayer, intercession, laughter, and tears, and just doing everyday things like shopping and putting together care packages for the homeless. Every one of those moments has been like a deposit into a heavenly bank account, and I have been stretched and increased in the process way beyond what I could ever imagine. The fruitfulness my husband Neil and I have experienced on a personal and professional level as a result of investing into Bella's life and ministry has been astonishing!

Her commitment to God is so profound, that although she has been overlooked and shoved to the side many times as someone insignificant, including by the church community, she has always remained steadfast and true to her calling. But Bella has never been abandoned or overlooked by God! I know just how much God delights in her every deed and is pleased with her life, which she lives in total surrender to Him.

Watching her sacrificial life has been a great inspiration to me and many others who have taken the time to get to know her. The best illustration of Bella's life that comes to mind is a massive umbrella that she is holding over a multitude of people. These include the homeless, the poor, the overlooked, the rejected, the orphans, the elderly, the single mothers, the handicapped, and many others in need of love and affection. I am certain that her life has touched so many people that her name is constantly mentioned in Heaven.

I believe that because of this unmatched level of commitment to God's heart, Bella has gained great favor and walks under an open Heaven. She has countless stories of encounters with God, where He has released to her revelations about eternity. She has also had numerous angelic visitations, and has received downloads of heavenly songs, which I believe someday will be a blessing to the masses here on Earth.

The encounter Bella had in 1983, when she went to visit Heaven for twenty-two hours during a coma in a hospital, was perhaps the most divine experience of her life. There are very profound keys that Jesus revealed to her during that tour, in which He also showed her Hell and the eternal torment that its inhabitants are doomed to endure.

It is by no accident that this book ended up in your hands. I hope you will be blessed, increased, and inspired as you read these pages filled with revelation of the afterlife. My prayer is that your mind will be transformed and your entire being reset as you fix your eyes on the most important thing that matters in this life—your eternity with God!

Neolla Hanekom
President, INTERNATIONAL OUTREACH MISSION, Inc.
www.internationaloutreachmission.org

"22 Hours – A Journey Through Eternity"

Glimpses of Things Unseen

By Bella Lamm

PART 1

___

CHAPTER 1

"Come!"— The Journey Begins

Deep down, we all instinctively know there is more. There is more than the success, money, and pleasures this world has to offer. In fact, there is no ending point for us; this life is merely the beginning. To some who have tasted the despair and pain of this life, that statement can seem hopeless and even terrifying. But it is great news for those who live by faith in Christ, for God has made a way for us to exchange our pain and sorrow for peace and hope that is available to us here on Earth, as well as for all of eternity! Knowing there is more to what is seen is the key to receiving this hope and freedom.

In 1983, I was admitted to what was then Balboa Hospital in San Diego, California for a hysterectomy. While I was in surgery, my blood count plummeted down to dangerous levels. Because of this, the doctor made the decision to close my body up, determining it was too risky to perform surgery; however, by that time my body had already entered into a coma.

Remarkably, I found myself above my body as my spirit was parting with it. I was speaking to the medical staff, "Hello! I am here. I am ok!" I persisted, "What are you doing? I'm fine!"

I even yanked the doctor's garment to get his attention and yelled, "Hey, doctor. I am ok. I am here!" I finally realized they could not see or hear me. I was astonished as I observed my body and the medical team. The members of the staff were busy trying to revive me, while simultaneously stitching up my stomach. I watched as they took my body to the Intensive Care Unit (ICU).

At that time of my life, I was married to my husband Edward Lake, who was an American serving in the military. We married in the Philippines in 1968, where I was born, and due to his service, eventually ended up moving to San Diego, California in 1981 as a military family. Two years later, I had to undergo the hysterectomy at age 33 after giving birth to my four children.

While watching my body in the ICU, I heard a voice say, "Come! I am taking you on a tour."[1] I did not respond or understand at first. Then the voice said it again, "Come! I am taking you on a tour." After hearing it once more, I was able to process and understand what was happening. I began to walk and suddenly found myself away from the hospital and in a tunnel unlike anything I had ever seen.

---

1 Revelation 22:17 (NKJV): And the Spirit and the bride say, "Come!" And let him who hears say, "Come!" And let him who thirsts come. Whoever desires, let him take the water of life freely.

It was translucent and surrounded by clouds of many different colors. In mere seconds, I was at the entrance to a beautiful gate.[2] A man of divine nature, who I later found out was Jesus Christ, was there holding out His hand to welcome me personally.

What was striking about this experience is that when this took place, I was not yet saved. It wasn't until three years later that I received Jesus Christ as my Lord and Savior.

In 1984, my family and I returned to Jacksonville, Florida, where I have lived ever since. I got divorced in 1985 and then remarried in 1986 to my second husband Jeffrey W. Lamm. Together, in 1986, we began attending Bethesda—an evangelical church. At that time, I was of the Catholic faith. I knew Jesus was Lord yet did not have a personal relationship with Him. Then, on Father's Day of that year, I got saved at Bethesda when I met Jesus Christ as my Lord and Savior. It was the happiest day of my life! The Bible says that Jesus is the only way to the Father. On that day, I not only accepted Jesus as my savior, but I became a daughter to my heavenly Father

Although I did not yet know Him personally, He welcomed me into Heaven in a most inviting way. I am overwhelmed as I reflect on this experience. It revealed so much about the nature of Jesus according to God's Word, which I was able to learn later through my personal relationship with Him since I became a Christian. Many of

---

2 Revelation 21:21 (NKJV): The twelve gates were twelve pearls: each individual gate was of one pearl. And the street of the city was pure gold, like transparent glass.

us are taught we need to be good enough in our actions to be loved by God. This could not be farther from the truth. In fact, Romans 5:8 (NKJV) clears this up by explaining, "But God demonstrates His own love toward us, in that while we were still sinners, Christ died for us." Yes, while I was still perishing in my sins, Christ already loved me and invited me to visit this beautiful place that I would one day call my home!

READER'S REFLECTIONS
(by AMBER PEÑA)

Jesus loves you and is listening when you come to Him.

1. *As you focus on Jesus, ask Him to remind you of the times He has invited you to come to Him and write them below.*

_____

_____

_____

_____

_____

_____

_____

_____

_____

_____

_____

2. *If you have not yet responded to His call, ask Him to forgive you of your sins and put your trust in how Jesus took your punishment upon Himself on the cross, then rose again 3 days later so you could be saved from the payment for your sin. Write your prayer below and trust that He hears you and is celebrating with all of Heaven over your choice to receive Him as your Savior and Lord! (see John 3:16; Romans 10:9-10)*

*Every thought that comes from Jesus will be confirmed through His written Word, so you can always use the Bible later to confirm His voice to your heart.

CHAPTER 2

His Hand in Mine

By the grace of God, there I stood at the entrance to Heaven, with Jesus by my side. In that moment He chose not to make Himself known to me as the Glorious Lord, but simply as a man who was welcoming and kind. I noticed that His hands had holes in them, and that fire gently emanated from the center of His hands. This is the moment I knew it was Jesus. His face was incredibly radiant, sweet, gentle, and loving. I was so overwhelmed by this encounter; there was no fear at all, only adoration.[3]

There are not enough words to describe the nature of Jesus! No one on Earth can even begin to compare because He has no equal. He made me feel like I was the only one in existence, yet He loves everyone the same. There is no partiality with Him. Jesus looked at me with the most wonderful and intense expression as He gave His

---

3 Revelation 1:13-16 (NKJV): and in the midst of the seven lampstands One like the Son of Man, clothed with a garment down to the feet and girded about the chest with a golden band. His head and hair were white like wool, as white as snow, and His eyes like a flame of fire; His feet were like fine brass, as if refined in a furnace, and His voice as the sound of many waters; He had in His right hand seven stars, out of His mouth went a sharp two-edged sword, and His countenance was like the sun shining in its strength.

hand to me and took mine into His. His skin was a dark caramel-brown, and His eyes were full of color—bluish-green and brownish-gold. Hand in hand, the Lord took me for a walk in Paradise.

Everything looked so magnificent! There were mountains and hills surrounded with glorious light sparkling everywhere. I somehow knew it had always had this look of a radiant morning filled with gentle and shimmering light. All my senses took in the beauty as I looked around. Even the temperature was pleasing. It was around sixty to sixty-five degrees Fahrenheit. A smell similar to the aroma of fresh roses filled the air. Trees playfully swayed in the breeze, creating a musical clapping sound. Birds beautifully harmonized, also lifting their praise to God. Flowers danced around, effortlessly showing their beauty.

I was filled with awe. A particular tree, which stood out to me, resembled the capital letter "Y." Just as I was admiring it, we went to sit underneath it. I knew deep down that this was the Tree of Life described in the book of Revelation, and I discerned that its name was "YAHWEH," the most revered name of God.

Sitting down underneath it, I noticed that the trees all over had beautiful, lush green leaves that never wither, and there were no dead leaves on the ground. This is when I asked Jesus, "Why is it that on Earth the plants wither, but here in Heaven they do not?"

He answered, "Don't you know? It is the sinful nature of people on Earth that causes the plants to wither as they take in every breath people exhale. This is how you know that the world is full of sin. It is what the earthly plants inhale that causes them to wither.

As we continued to sit and gaze at the magnificent views all around, I observed a strong water stream beside us, rolling passionately. I had a desire to look into the water, hoping to see a river rock or a stone; however, upon looking, I noticed that instead of rocks, there were brilliant, sparkling gemstones. What a sight![4]

This glorious moment and place reminded me of Psalm 23, which says that the Lord is my shepherd who "makes me to lie down in green pastures" and "leads me beside the still waters." I have lived through much hardship in my life—first in the Philippines as a child in the wake of the Japanese war, then in America as an adult. Much of the hardship I experienced was due to lack of parental guidance and having too many responsibilities growing up, such as taking care of many children in my family. Who I am today would not be possible without His grace carrying me through. I can truly say that He continually restores my soul in the way that only He can.

---

4 Revelation 22:1-2 (NKJV): And he showed me a pure river of water of life, clear as crystal, proceeding from the throne of God and of the Lamb. In the middle of its street, and on either side of the river, *was* the tree of life, which bore twelve fruits, each *tree* yielding its fruit every month. The leaves of the tree *were* for the healing of the nations.

READER'S REFLECTIONS
(by AMBER PEÑA)

When we look at Jesus with adoration, all fear vanishes!

1. *Ask the Lord to show you an area in your life where your focus can shift from fear to Him and write it below.*

_____
_____
_____
_____
_____
_____
_____
_____
_____
_____
_____
_____
_____
_____
_____
_____

2. *What are some things about Jesus that outshines the fear in this situation? Write about this area of God's character below and allow yourself to become in awe of Him. (For example, His healing power, His protection, His provision, etc.)*

Every thought that comes from Jesus will be confirmed through His written Word, so you can always use the Bible later to confirm His voice to your heart.

CHAPTER 3

Jesus Loves the Little Children

While sitting under that beautiful "Y" tree and taking in all the beauty of Paradise, I suddenly began to see movement as children started coming out of nowhere. They were so lively and playful. When they saw the Lord, they ran toward Him, joyfully tackling Him to the ground! The Lord Jesus opened His arms inviting each of them to receive all the love and hugs they wanted. They instinctively knew to take turns by creating an order of five or six children giving Jesus hugs one at a time, while the others patiently anticipated getting their embraces. They all received so much love and were having so much fun. Laughter and delight were all around. They were enjoying every bit of their time with Jesus, screaming with loud, joyful voices. I somehow knew that these were children who had not experienced this kind of love on Earth. They were the unwanted ones, but they were not abandoned by the Lord! His open arms were wholly offered to every one of them. Surely, without a doubt, He has always had angels surround and watch over them during their lives on Earth.[5]

This moment reminds me of the time during my childhood when I experienced playing outside with a boy who would occasionally appear to come play with me. He was wearing short pants and a Spalding-type shirt. I was playing around with Him like I would with a normal child, without even giving it a second thought. He was so cute playing and interacting with me, but when we would play hide and seek, He would disappear and would not be found anywhere. The same thing happened over and over again. I thought that perhaps it was a ghost. Later in life, I understood that this boy was Jesus.

I also recall another unusual childhood experience. One night while I was asleep, three angels carried me out to the top of the roof, and they sat and talked with me. I have no recollection of those conversations, except for the fact that I was taken up during my sleep to talk with them.

I began to hear God's voice at a very young age, although I did not yet know Him personally. I believe the Holy Spirit was with me all along. I did not understand

---

5 Matthew 19:14 (NKJV): But Jesus said, "Let the little children come to Me, and do not forbid them; for of such is the kingdom of heaven."

Mark 10:15-16 (NKJV): Assuredly, I say to you, whoever does not receive the kingdom of God as a little child will by no means enter it." And He took them up in His arms, laid *His* hands on them, and blessed them.

why I heard voices, thinking I must be crazy. At age five I heard a voice saying, "American!" I wondered, "What is American?" That stayed in my memory. Little did I know I was an American citizen on my mother's side.

My father left my mother when she was 7 months pregnant with me. During that time, there was a fire in our house—located in the mountain province of Banaue—which destroyed the upstairs living area and the downstairs grocery store. As a result of that tragic experience, she developed amnesia. Due to her illness, my mother and I were never able to have a meaningful relationship, and I felt deprived of her love and care all through my childhood.

Even though it was not until age 36 that I received salvation in Christ, He was waiting for me all along with arms wide open, like those He offered to the children in Paradise. I finally gave my life to the Lord on Father's Day of 1986 by saying, "Lord, I am not worthy! But if You can accept me for who I am, I offer myself to You as my Lord and Savior!" I thank my Lord Jesus for being so gentle, kind, and loving. He was able to fill every void I had ever felt and gave me the love and affection that I never received from my parents. God's love for each person is endless, with no beginning and no end. He longs for each one to come to Him and opens His arms to us all.[6]

---

6 Jeremiah 31:3 (NKJV): The LORD has appeared of old to me, *saying*: / "Yes, I have loved you with an everlasting love; / Therefore with lovingkindness I have drawn you."

Romans 10:9-10 (NKJV): ...if you confess with your mouth the Lord Jesus and believe in your heart that God has raised Him from the dead, you will be saved. For with the heart one believes unto righteousness, and with the mouth confession is made unto salvation.

READER'S REFLECTIONS
(by AMBER PEÑA)

Jesus is always so close! He is longing to protect, heal, and bring you joy.

1. *Ask the Lord where He is right now with you as you pay attention to His gentle voice with your heart. What facial expression is He making? What does He have to say to you about His love for you? Write the spontaneous thoughts that light up on your mind as you fix your attention on Him. (His voice will always match His loving words of the Bible.)*

_____

_____

_____

_____

_____

_____

_____

_____

_____

_____

_____

_____

_____

_____

_____

*Every thought that comes from Jesus will be confirmed through His written Word, so you can always use the Bible later to confirm His voice to your heart.

CHAPTER 4

"Come Up to The Mountain!" No Turning Back

At one point, I found myself walking alone but still sensing the closeness of the Lord. Then, suddenly, I heard a voice calling me. "Come up to the mountain," the powerful voice of the Father God resounded.[7] The mountain was very high and majestic.[8] As I began walking up to the top, the voice declared instructions, "Come up and sit on the stair number thirteen." I wondered to myself, "Why do I need to sit on number thirteen? What is wrong

---

7 Ephesians 2:18 (NKJV): For through Him [Christ] we both have access by one Spirit unto the Father (God).

8 Isaiah 2:2-3 (NKJV): Now it shall come to pass in the latter days / That the mountain of the Lord's house / Shall be established on the top of the mountains, / And shall be exalted above the hills; / And all nations shall flow to it. / Many people shall come and say, / "Come, and let us go up to the mountain of the Lord, / To the house of the God of Jacob…"

Exodus 24:12 (NKJV): Then the Lord said to Moses, "Come up to Me on the mountain and be there; and I will give you tablets of stone, and the law and commandments which I have written, that you may teach them."

with number one?" In that moment I thought to myself, "I must still be human in order to have thoughts like these." This is when I realized that I was just a visitor; I wasn't completely like the rest of them who were there.

The road was narrow and very steep on the sides. I looked down and saw dark green trees of all sizes. I remember feeling a little bit worried that I might fall off while climbing these great mountain stairs, once again revealing my just being a visitor with fleshly thoughts. At the same time, though, I was also filled with admiration and wonder as I climbed higher. I could see countless beautiful mansions, which sparkled like topaz! After a long walk up, I noticed the twelve apostles sitting on the top twelve stairs. I could tell they were awaiting my arrival at the top, because they were looking around with warm smiles, in anticipation to welcome me.

This is the mountain of The Lord, referred to throughout the Bible. It is the highest place one can achieve in the spirit realm, yet it is available to us while on Earth through a personal relationship with Jesus. At the top of the mountain, there was a beautiful gate made of sparkling gold, and on both sides of the gate were standing live golden lions with golden crowns on their heads, and I discerned that the two lions symbolized the Father and the Son. So majestic and awe-inspiring! Jesus was waiting for me on the other side.

When I entered the gate and looked behind me, I realized that everywhere the Lord and I had walked disappeared. Even the steps vanished. There was no option to turn back.

I said to Jesus, "Why is there no trace of the road behind us to go back? Everything vanished."

The Lord answered me and said, "Uninvited spirits are not welcome. They are unable to come in."[9]

I did not quite understand fully what the Lord had said, so I simply decided to just trust Him because His ways and thoughts are so much higher than mine. We went through long hallways, and the walls simply closed behind us, reminding me that there was no turning back when I follow the Lord. As I looked forward, there was so much beauty, peace, and stillness.

---

9 Revelation 21:27 (NKJV): But there shall by no means enter it anything that defiles, or causes an abomination or a lie, but only those who are written in the Lamb's Book of Life.

READER'S REFLECTIONS
(by AMBER PEÑA)

We all face the choice to answer the Lord's call to come up higher. He says in Romans 12:9 to hate what is evil and to cling to what is good.

1. *What are some areas in your life that you sense God's loving conviction to leave behind in order to come up higher and obey His voice? Write them below as you sense His desire for your freedom in every area.*

_____

_____

_____

_____

_____

_____

_____

_____

_____

_____

_____

_____

_____

_____

_____

_____

Every thought that comes from Jesus will be confirmed through His written Word, so you can always use the Bible later to confirm His voice to your heart.

CHAPTER 5

Special Access – Life on Earth Matters

As Jesus and I continued to walk together, I instinctively knew I was only permitted to see certain parts of the gorgeous creation around me. Everything else was concealed, which only the angels and "ranking" saints could see and enter into. Yes, there are ranks among the saints in Heaven, as confirmed by the twenty-four elders who surround the throne of God and worship Him by casting their golden crowns at His feet.

As Jesus and I were walking from place to place, I noticed an area that was open to all the saints. It was a glorious place where all joined in loud worship to our Master, our Lord, and King of Kings! They were free to worship and to have time with the Lord as they looked up and adored Him.

One of the most significant things I was able to notice is that every saint in Heaven is young. Their vibrant youth is restored regardless of their age at the time they died on Earth! I thought that was so remarkable. The only ones who appeared old were the twenty-four elders, and I presumed that was due to their ranking.

I also saw that all the saints could walk around the outer courtyard, which was adorned with beautiful columns and had magnificent walls. There were several things to see all around, like saints with their families enjoying the beauty of the Holy Place and spending time with each other, walking, and enjoying delicious fruits and food served by angels. The food looked amazing. Another thing that stood out to me was how there was manna and grapes the size of plums![10]

I perceived that angels were always diligently serving the saints, both in Heaven and on Earth. I also understood that one way they do this on Earth is by delivering answered prayers. Our prayers are being answered by God and then are delivered by the angels.[11] Some may think, *My prayers have not been answered*, or, *My prayers have not even been heard*. But these thoughts are not true if you pray in faith. Yes, the Lord hears our prayers! But only if we believe. When we ask in faith for our desires and needs to be met, we can be sure that our prayers have been heard. We can be sure that our prayers have been

---

10 Psalm 78:23-25 (NKJV): Yet He had commanded the clouds above, / and opened the doors of heaven, / had rained down manna on them to eat, / and given them of the bread of heaven. / Men ate angels' food; / He sent them food to the full.

Revelation 2:17 (NKJV): "He who has an ear, let him hear what the Spirit says to the churches. To him who overcomes I will give some of the hidden manna to eat."

11 Hebrews 1:14 (NKJV): Are they not all ministering spirits sent forth to minister for those who will inherit salvation?

answered. But when we take back what we have already given to Him, then we no longer have faith in what He can do. We are trusting in ourselves rather than in God and are carrying the load on our shoulders instead of letting God carry it. It requires faith to receive the answered prayers that have been delivered. This is what happens within the process of your prayers. Answered prayers take faith to receive.[12]

I have experienced this truth in action many times in my life. One example of this is when I did not have enough money to pay my bills sometime after this encounter in Heaven. My water was going to be shut off on Monday morning, but in faith, I lifted up my bill and said, "Lord, I know You will take care of this bill!"

Only half an hour later, I was at a Gate gas station with just $11 for my gas. I felt an abrupt and strong tap on my knee three times. Then I heard a voice say, "Look down!" When I did, I saw a $100 bill right on my foot—a brand new bill that had not yet been in circulation! Not only did it pay the $89 needed for my water bill, but it was an additional $11. I now had $22 for my gas to take a journey in my car and to highlight the twenty-two-hour journey that I had experienced in Heaven with the Lord.

It was a direct answer to prayer which I had lifted to God in faith. He answered that prayer, and the angels were

---

12 Hebrews 11:1-3 (NKJV): Now faith is the substance of things hoped for, the evidence of things not seen. For by it the elders obtained a good testimony. By faith we understand that the worlds were framed by the word of God, so that the things which are seen were not made of things which are visible.

Hebrews 4:16 (NKJV): Let us therefore come boldly to the throne of grace, that we may obtain mercy and find grace to help in time of need.

quickly sent on their assignment to deliver that answer to me. I knew God would not fail me! This is what faith is all about: trusting in His faithfulness.[13] Just remember that our Lord is good! He has never forgotten you. Anything you ask in His name with faith, believing He will answer, will be given to you![14]

---

13 Deuteronomy 7:9 (NKJV): Therefore know that the Lord your God, He is God, the faithful God who keeps covenant and mercy for a thousand generations with those who love Him and keep His commandments.

14 Matthew 21:22 (NKJV): And whatever things you ask in prayer, believing, you will receive.

Mark 11:22 (NKJV): So Jesus answered and said to them, "Have faith in God."

Ephesians 3:12 (NKJV): …in whom we have boldness and access with confidence through faith in Him.

READER'S REFLECTIONS
(by AMBER PEÑA)

It's easy to trust in ourselves for provision, but God's Word shows us His heart in this area. He says in Philippians 4:19 (NKJV), "...And my God shall supply all your need according to His riches in glory by Christ Jesus."

1. *As you turn your attention to Jesus, ask God to show you an area in your life that you can trust Him for provision in.*

2. *Write out a prayer of faith to Jesus and ask Him to provide for you and to show you His heart of joy towards you as you place your trust in Him.*

_____

_____

_____

_____

_____

_____

_____

_____

_____

_____

_____

_____

_____

*Every thought that comes from Jesus will be confirmed through His written Word, so you can always use the Bible later to confirm His voice to your heart.

"22 Hours – A Journey Through Eternity"

Glimpses of Things Unseen

By Bella Lamm

PART 2

———

CHAPTER 6

In My Father's House Are Many Mansions

Jesus and I continued to walk through the outer courtyard. Many of the buildings were tall, with the outside walls resembling a clear, sparkling topaz. Oh, the beauty of those mansions! I could see through them and noticed the inside of each one was embellished with breathtaking gold, surrounded by brilliant sparkling light. I noticed that the streets were gold as well.[15] We were surrounded by beautiful trees, colorful flowers, and soft grass. Everything looked so well-manicured and adorned with excellence. There is nothing on Earth that compares to what I saw. I took it all in and cherished how it consistently seemed like a refreshing spring morning.

---

15 Revelation 21:18-25 (NKJV): The construction of its wall was of jasper; and the city was pure gold, like clear glass. The foundations of the wall of the city were adorned with all kinds of precious stones: the first foundation was jasper, the second sapphire, the third chalcedony, the fourth emerald, the fifth sardonyx, the sixth sardius, the seventh chrysolite, the eighth beryl, the ninth topaz, the tenth chrysoprase, the eleventh jacinth, and the twelfth amethyst. The twelve gates were twelve pearls: each individual gate was of one pearl. And the street of the city was pure gold, like transparent glass.

There were souls there that the Lord called the "grace saints." I noticed that they lived in smaller dwellings that resembled one-story duplexes or storage rooms. I asked Jesus what these smaller dwellings represented. He explained that they were for the saints who accepted Him on Earth, but who never did anything for Him or His Kingdom. He told me how materials for a person's mansion are actually brought in each time a person serves Him. He continued with love and expounded, "If you serve Me, the materials will be added to build your house each time you serve. Your material then builds up your mansion!"[16] He kindly mentioned how the grace saints had the materials available to them to further expand their buildings, but no additional understanding or explanation was given to me at that moment.

Another thing I noticed about these grace saints was how they were not welcome to go freely into a place that was unseen by them; only those invited could see it and enter in. It was clear to me that those who served the Lord were indeed rewarded for their sacrifice and efforts to Him. As I pondered on this, I looked and saw the house of Mother Theresa. Her name was on the doorpost outside. At that time, she was still alive on Earth but had already done much to serve God by caring for the poor.

Not long after, I saw my own mansion, which had seven

---

16 Hebrews 6:10 (NKJV): For God is not unjust to forget your work and labor of love which you have shown toward His name, in that you have ministered to the saints, and do minister.

Revelation 22:12 (NKJV): And behold, I am coming quickly, and My reward is with Me, to give to every one according to his work.

rooms.[17] The first door led into the living room, and as I entered that door, there was a vast open area, resembling a resort or a recreational center. There were two pools, a large one and a small one, with running water coming down through the wall like a majestic mountain-waterfall! The larger waterfall on one side and the smaller one on the other side. The walls were made up of natural rock that resembled big golden nuggets sparkling through the crystal-clear water. There was no electricity, no electric plugs, no cooking, no stove. Everything was illuminated by the light of God's Glory! A truly amazing place!

The Lord then guided me upstairs. The first room, my bedroom, was indeed enormous and decorated with light purple chiffon-like material. It was very lovely, resembling a princess's room. The other six bedrooms were large rooms filled with children and adults of all ages.[18] I did not expect to see so many people in these guest rooms! "Who are these people, Lord?" I asked, not recognizing any of them.

He answered me, "These are the people you have helped! These are the ones you have cared for, clothed, fed, and given guidance to."

"Wow, so many!" I thought. I believe that the many people who filled the rooms of my heavenly mansion reflect those whom Jesus so dearly loves and whom I have

---

17 John 14:2 (NKJV): In My Father's house are many mansions; if it were not so, I would have told you. I go to prepare a place for you.

18 Matthew 18:3-6 (NKJV): Assuredly, I say to you, unless you are converted and become as little children, you will by no means enter the kingdom of heaven. Therefore whoever humbles himself as this little child is the greatest in the kingdom of heaven. Whoever receives one little child like this in My name receives Me.

the privilege of serving here on Earth. The mansion itself was so huge, each room being at least thirty-five by forty feet in size. I was just overwhelmed by the size of each room, and everything was surrounded by translucent gold walls. The outside of the mansion appeared to be made of topaz and sparkling, transparent gold.

I find it very interesting that Jesus decided to show me Mother Theresa's mansion in Heaven, and I know now it had a specific purpose. Ever since I was very young, I have felt a connection with Mother Theresa. I believe her mantle was passed on to me. I began serving the poor and taking care of the needy myself at a very young age. In fact, in 1962, at only twelve years of age, I was already gladly caring for five of my little cousins who had been orphaned.

At that time, I had very little knowledge of my family's life history. It was not until 2016, when my great-aunt shared my great-grandfather's story, along with pictures on social media, that I was able to learn of our family's heritage. My great-aunt shared that my great-grandfather was serving God as a Methodist pastor. I also discovered that my great-grandmother became a widow during the Japanese war, but I did not learn about my great-grandfather's background and history until 2016. I was not able to meet him, but I can see how intertwined the calling of God on my life is with that of my great-grandfather's. I only heard of it after having served the homeless in downtown Jacksonville, Florida for two years, since 2014. I was very pleasantly surprised to find out that it is in our family's bloodline to serve the poor so generously! All throughout my life I have enjoyed helping the poor and the children. I believe the rooms that I saw in my heavenly mansion that were filled with children reflect these children whom Jesus so dearly loves, and whom I have the privilege of serving here on Earth.

Reflecting on the magnitude and beauty of those mansions and the revelation I received about what it took to build them, things have become so much clearer. I am reminded from God's word that it is not just any works that accomplish the construction of our dwellings in Heaven. It is the "good works" referred to in Ephesians 2:10, which God has prepared beforehand for His workmanship, His children, to walk in. Many people throughout history have achieved good works, but the revelation that God has imparted to me is that the only way those works glorify God and carry eternal value is if they are done by the leading of the Holy Spirit. The only way we can be led by the Holy Spirit is when we are children of God through Jesus Christ, and through Him alone. This is the key to gathering materials to build our mansions in Heaven. I believe this also speaks of spending our time wisely on Earth to accomplish only the things which God calls us to do; nothing more and nothing less. This is the only way our lives will be meaningful and fulfilling. It is also the only way our heavenly homes will be constructed according to God's design. What a beautiful revelation!

READER'S REFLECTIONS
(by AMBER PEÑA)

Serving the unfortunate is so dear to the heart of God that He honors His children for all of eternity when we help the poor, hungry, imprisoned, and outcasts.

1. *Ask the Lord to help you begin to sense His heart for the unfortunate today.*

2. *Ask the Lord to highlight in your thoughts a way you can serve Him by serving someone who needs His love. Write it down and act on His prompting with all your heart.*

_____
_____
_____
_____
_____
_____
_____
_____
_____
_____
_____
_____
_____
_____
_____
_____

*Every thought that comes from Jesus will be confirmed through His written Word, so you can always use the Bible later to confirm His voice to your heart.

CHAPTER 7

Your Life is Recorded in Heaven

As I looked around, I noticed a beautiful, wide-flowing river with shimmering, living water. This gently flowing water seemed to be the source of the rushing stream I had seen earlier. This water had stunning gemstones inside of it like the other. It was gracefully releasing a soothing sound.[19] I took the moment in and once again treasured the sounds of the peaceful water, the playful trees, the sweet birds, and the pleasant animals. The trees continued to sing with their clapping sounds, and the birds were still serenading.[20] This time I also noticed how the animals looked at me from far off with a sweet look in their eyes and soft, joyful sounds as if they wanted to play with me. There were many different kinds of animals, even including

---

19 Revelation 22:1 (NKJV): And he showed me a pure river of water of life, clear as crystal, proceeding from the throne of God and of the Lamb.

20 Isaiah 55:12 (NKJV): For you shall go out with joy, / and be led out with peace; / the mountains and the hills shall / break forth into singing before you, / and all the trees of the field shall clap their hands.

beautiful unicorns.[21] I also noticed fruit trees unlike any I had seen on Earth. I was amazed by the surroundings and remember wondering why Earth was not full of this level of beauty. It was so excellent. Everything around me was full of life!

Shortly after, we went inside one of many warehouses. I saw body parts ready to be put together and angels busy at work. They were making sure that the answers to people's prayers of faith were being delivered. These organs and body parts, along with houses, cars, and so much more are constantly being delivered to people who pray to God in faith.[22]

Next, I saw a long hallway. When we passed through the hallway, I noticed once again that the buildings and everything else behind us closed in—vanished. As we came through the hallway into a room, I observed how everything inside was made of shimmering gold! Only those invited to come in were able to enter, which depended on their ranking. This ranking also applied to the angels. Only certain areas were visible to me in this room.

After this, we entered another awe-inspiring room, in which was the Book of Life! I was shown how everyone has his or her own name, and that the Book of

---

21 Isaiah 65:25 (NKJV): "The wolf and the lamb shall feed together, / the lion shall eat straw like the ox, / and dust shall be the serpent's food. / They shall not hurt nor destroy in all My holy mountain," / says the LORD.

22 Psalm 103:20 (NKJV): Bless the LORD, you His angels, / who excel in strength, who do His word, / heeding the voice of His word.

Life revealseach of our lives completely.[23] There were shelves that contained all the names in order. Each person will see him- or herself on a large screen, watching his or her life from the time of birth until death.

I have heard of many accounts of people sharing this type of experience while on Earth. In many cases this happens while people have a near-death experience, where time and space seize to exist, and they find themselves before a large screen watching their whole lives replayed before their eyes. This same screen is what I saw in Heaven. If there is ever a doubt in your heart whether God is aware of your life or if what you do is noticed, remember these words: everything you do, even to the smallest details of your life, is recorded in Heaven. Nothing is hidden from God's all-seeing eyes! Therefore, know that He loves you and live your life in a way that honors and pleases Him.

After I was shown this, we went to another room where I saw many bottles of tears. Some were overflowing with tears, while some only had a few drops. Some bottles were even empty. All the tears that were shed while calling on the name of the Lord were stored here. If we pour out our hearts unto the Lord, He hears our prayers and saves our tears. These tears are very precious to Him.[24]

---

23 Revelation 3:5 (NKJV): He who overcomes shall be clothed in white garments, and I will not blot out his name from the Book of Life; but I will confess his name before My Father and before His angels.

Luke 10:20 (NKJV): Nevertheless do not rejoice in this, that the spirits are subject to you, but rather rejoice because your names are written in heaven.

24 Psalm 56:8 (NKJV): You number my wanderings; / put my tears into Your bottle; / are they not in Your book?

Revelation 21:4 (NKJV): And God will wipe away every tear from their eyes; there shall be no more death, nor sorrow, nor crying. There shall be no more pain, for the former things have passed away.

How encouraging it is to know that God keeps a record of everything in our lives! Not only does God designate a special room to store our tears in bottles, but according to Psalm 56:8, they also get recorded in a book. This means that He keeps track of all our suffering, pain, and moments of weakness when we cry out to Him for help, so that one day He can reward us with abundant joy and peace for choosing to be faithful to Him during those times.

I have cried so many tears in my own life, that my heavenly bottles are probably overflowing. Most of those were shed privately, without anyone being aware. Yet I am comforted with the knowledge that God has seen each one and has turned those countless tears into great joy when He has met me in my despair over and over. He has not once abandoned me, and I know He will do the same for you if you choose to put your trust in Him.

READER'S REFLECTIONS
(by AMBER PEÑA)

Jesus is full of love for you. If we pour out our heart unto the Lord, He hears our prayers and saves our tears.

1. *Think of an area in your life that you might feel sad, let down, confused, or even bitter about.*

2. *Ask the Lord to help you pour out your heart to Him about it and spend time writing a prayer to Him about it.*

3. *Focus on His love for you and ask Him what He has to say to you about this. Pay attention to the thoughts that light up on your mind as you focus on Him and write them down.*

_____

_____

_____

_____

_____

_____

_____

_____

_____

_____

_____

_____

_____

_____

*Every thought that comes from Jesus will be confirmed through His written Word, so you can always use the Bible later to confirm His voice to your heart.

CHAPTER 8

Hell is A Real Place. How Do I Avoid It?

The Lord Jesus also took me to visit Hell. I was on His right side. Hell was such a terrifying place. While we were there, I was very anxious about what the Lord might say to me. I was afraid He would say something like how Hell was where I belonged. "All these people had done wrong, and this is where they belong," the Lord said.

Wow, I was so nervous, just waiting for Him to say something about me. I saw a lot of faces that I recognized: famous people like pop stars, nuns, popes, and even pastors, as well as people I knew personally who had died.[25] One lady stood out to me the most. She was from my hometown in the Philippines and was an elder in our town. I remembered how she would smile when I saw her in town. She was never rough—just a nice young lady. I was so shocked to see her in Hell! I thought of how we

---

25 Matthew 7:13 (NKJV): Enter by the narrow gate; for wide is the gate and broad is the way that leads to destruction, and there are many who go in by it.

knew each other as kids, playing in my old neighborhood. This lady was sweet, but now she was yelling for help: screaming for relief. "Please! Please!" She yelled it over and over many times, begging for help. "Can't you hear me?" she screamed.

Everywhere I looked was an ocean of fire with loud, boiling lava. There were many loud voices crying for help. The smell was also overwhelming, similar to pungent sulfur. The bubbling fire was everywhere. Their screams seemed so far away, and I knew that no one could hear them except the ranking demons that came and tormented them with their spears or with whatever level of torture they deserved.[26] "Please!" the loud voice of the lady continued to beg for help. "Is anyone there? Can't you hear me? Please, help me!" She was pleading for help, yet no one could hear her. She was unable to do anything.

I yanked the Lord's garment and asked Him, "Can't You please help her?"

The Lord said sorrowfully, "It's too late."[27]

His response made me incredibly miserable. I began crying, tears rolling profusely down my face. I could not

---

26 Revelation 20:13-16 (NKJV): The sea gave up the dead who were in it, and Death and Hades delivered up the dead who were in them. And they were judged, each one according to his works. Then Death and Hades were cast into the lake of fire. This is the second death. And anyone not found written in the Book of Life was cast into the lake of fire.

27 Luke 16:24-26 (NKJV) "Then he cried and said, 'Father Abraham, have mercy on me, and send Lazarus that he may dip the tip of his finger in water and cool my tongue; for I am tormented in this flame.' But Abraham said, 'Son, remember that in your lifetime you received your good things, and likewise Lazarus evil things; but now he is comforted and you are tormented. And besides all this, between us and you there is a great gulf fixed, so that those who want to pass from here to you cannot, nor can those from there pass to us.'"

help but weep, "Oh no!" I reflected on how I knew this person at a young age and how sweet and considerate she was, always with a smiling face, as far back as I could remember. And now, there was no way out! She was not given another chance at all. She had no hope. There were so many just like her, and they all were unbelievably tormented. I felt utterly helpless because nothing could be done. Thank God forever and ever that I now have confidence that Hell is not the place for me, because I surrendered my life to Him and received His payment for my sin![28]

Being there in that place, I was unsure what to expect. There was no way out, and I had not yet received Jesus' gift of paying for my sin on the cross. Only by God's grace was I given the chance to be sent back, so I could repent of my sin and accept Him as my Savior. He empowered me to change my ways after I became a new creation in Him! There is no way out for any person except through Jesus Christ, by accepting Him as our Lord and Savior and turning our back on sin.[29] I pray that each person reading this finds the joy of truth. I am so grateful that I was given the chance to go back and seek our Lord! Even though it took me three years after this experience to understand what Jesus has done for me and for all of us,

---

28 Matthew 16:24-27 (NKJV): If anyone desires to come after Me, let him deny himself, and take up his cross, and follow Me. For whoever desires to save his life will lose it, but whoever loses his life for My sake will find it. For what profit is it to a man if he gains the whole world, and loses his own soul? Or what will a man give in exchange for his soul? For the Son of Man will come in the glory of His Father with His angels, and then He will reward each according to his works.

29 John 14:6 (NKJV): Jesus said to him, "I am the way, the truth, and the life. No one comes to the Father except through Me."

and to offer myself to the Lord, I am now fully redeemed by His grace! I am free! "Thank You, Lord Jesus!" I say, "Thank You, Lord!"[30]

---

30 Philippians 4:4-5 (NKJV): Rejoice in the Lord always. Again I will say, rejoice! Let your gentleness be known to all men. The Lord is at hand.

READER'S REFLECTIONS
(by AMBER PEÑA)

John 14:6 (NKJV) says, "Jesus said to him, 'I am the way, the truth, and the life. No one comes to the Father except through Me.'" I experienced the truth of this verse. Every soul is destined for eternal punishment unless they receive the One who paid the eternal price for our sin. We cannot be received into Heaven any other way except through Jesus.

1. *Quiet yourself down, fix your eyes on Jesus, and ask Him if there is anything other than Him that you are trusting in to get into Heaven. As you keep your focus on Him and His love for you, write down any thoughts that light up in your mind.*

2. *Focus on His love for you and ask Him what He has to say to you about this. Pay attention to the thoughts that light up on your mind as you focus on Him and write them down.*

_____
_____
_____
_____
_____
_____
_____
_____

Every thought that comes from Jesus will be confirmed through His written Word, so you can always use the Bible later to confirm His voice to your heart.

"22 Hours – A Journey Through Eternity"

Glimpses of Things Unseen

By Bella Lamm

PART 3

CHAPTER 9

The Throne Room

After visiting Hell, I was taken to see the throne of God and watched as the Lord Jesus sat down at the right hand of God the Father.[31] Oh, how marvelous the Lord looked with His gold crown resting on His head! This is the moment when He revealed Himself as the King of Kings and the Lord of Lords who reigns forever!

I once more reflected on my journey. I was able to see how the saints sang to the Lord everywhere in Heaven. They sang out loud in the courtyard as we walked from place to place and now here in the throne room of God. Listening to their endless praise, I was in awe of how beautifully they sounded. I also listened to the angels' worship and watched how they continually moved and served, and how the twenty-four elders knelt down before

---

31 1 Kings 22:19 (NKJV): Then Micaiah said, "Therefore hear the word of the LORD: I saw the LORD sitting on His throne, and all the host of heaven standing by, on His right hand and on His left."

Acts 7:49 (NKJV): "Heaven is My throne, and earth is My footstool…"

the throne.[32] In fact, the book of Revelation tells us that these twenty-four elders continually fall on their faces before God and cast their crowns before His throne in adoration. They do not hold on to their crowns, which God chose to place on their heads as a reward for their service to Him on Earth. Instead, they offer their crowns back to God as a form of worship. What a picture of humility and selfless worship to God, which we are also called to offer Him while living here on Earth. When you know God intimately, you cannot help but worship and adore Him this way!

I also noticed how the saints were clothed with sashes of various colors wrapped around their waists to show their ranking. Some of the colors I noticed were soft yellow, soft purple, soft pink, blue, and gold. While I took in all the beauty and splendor around me, I felt myself waiting for Him to say something about me. In fact, I felt this the entire time we were on the tour, but He remained consistent with His mission to show me all that He wanted to show me. While in the throne room, I could sense that it was almost time for Him to send me back.

I continued to reflect on all I had seen and experienced, such as that beautiful white unicorn and so many different animals that I enjoyed playing with. I thought about how much I enjoyed being surrounded with so much love and

---

32 Revelation 4:10-11 (NKJV): The twenty-four elders fall down before Him who sits on the throne and worship Him who lives forever and ever, and cast their crowns before the throne, saying: "You are worthy, O Lord, / to receive glory and honor and power; / for You created all things, / and by Your will they exist and were created."

Revelation 7:11 (NKJV): All the angels stood around the throne and the elders and the four living creatures, and fell on their faces before the throne and worshiped God...

peace. It was similar to being in the secret place with the Lord, which is available for all to enter into while here on Earth, because of Jesus' sacrifice on the cross.[33] I felt like I never wanted to leave, but at the same time I grew anxious about my children who were left behind. I knew they needed me. My motherly duties and responsibilities compelled me to desire to go back. I asked Him, "Lord, how about my children?" I was concerned and even began to feel panic because I felt anxious to get back home to my kids. I was not sure how long I had been there or even if my life on Earth was over, so I begged Him to send me back to them. He said to me with love in His eyes, "I understand." He put His hand on my head, and at that moment I could sense how much He loved my company.[34] I cried out for my children once again, and the Lord sent me back home to them.

Visiting Heaven for twenty-two hours was the most divine experience I have ever had in my life! I realize now that God invited me on that journey to entrust me with the duty of sharing the reality of His heavenly kingdom here

---

33 Psalm 91:1 (NKJV): He who dwells in the secret place of the Most High / shall abide under the shadow of the Almighty.

Matthew 6:6 (NKJV): But you, when you pray, go into your room, and when you have shut your door, pray to your Father who is in the secret place; and your Father who sees in secret will reward you openly.

Psalm 23:1-3 (NKJV): The Lord *is* my shepherd; / I shall not want. / He makes me to lie down in green pastures; / He leads me beside the still waters. / He restores my soul...

34 Romans 8:38-39 (NKJV): For I am persuaded that neither death nor life, nor angels nor principalities nor powers, nor things present nor things to come, nor height nor depth, nor any other created thing, shall be able to separate us from the love of God which is in Christ Jesus our Lord.

Ephesians 3:18-19 (NKJV): May be able to comprehend with all the saints what is the width and length and depth and height—to know the love of Christ which passes knowledge; that you may be filled with all the fullness of God.

on Earth. That is the reason He allowed me to come back to my earthly dwelling. Only by God's grace was I sent back, because had I stayed, I would have certainly ended up spending eternity in Hell.

I do not fully understand why it took me so long to surrender my life to Jesus after that experience. Perhaps I was too set in my ways and in my Catholic religion. I am so grateful to God for setting me free from that bondage three years later, so I could come to Him and call Him Savior of my life!

READER'S REFLECTIONS
(by AMBER PEÑA)

Jesus is full of majesty and glory! He is worthy of all the praise He receives in the throne room and so much more.

1. *Ask the Lord to show you a glimpse of His glory and majesty as you focus all your attention on the depths of His love for you and for all He's done for you. Pay attention to any pictures or thoughts that light up on your mind and write them down.*

_____

_____

_____

_____

_____

_____

_____

2. *Spend a few minutes joining in with the worship of Heaven and tell Jesus how wonderful He is. Write your praise to Him, speak it aloud to Him, and/or sing it to Him.*

_____

_____

_____

_____

_____

_____

_____

Every thought that comes from Jesus will be confirmed through His written Word, so you can always use the Bible later to confirm His voice to your heart.

CHAPTER 10

Your Assignment on Earth is Not Over!

Heaven's Invitation to A Higher Purpose

After making my request known to God in the throne room, I found myself back in the hospital room with my spirit back in my body. I was crying, "I am ok; I am here!"

The smiling nurse said, "Where have you been the last twenty-two hours? You were in a coma. We weren't sure you would make it."

As I looked around, they were all smiling with joy. They told me they were about to administer a painkiller because of my surgery, but I said, "No, I went to Heaven!" I insisted on delaying to take the anesthetic, so I could take that opportunity to tell them what had happened. I cried aloud and spoke to all of them who were ready to hear my story. I enjoyed remembering and sharing how beautiful Heaven is, and I could see delight on their faces as they listened.[35]

After much excitement and telling so many about my divine experience, I finally got some rest for a few days. Even as I rested, I kept reflecting on all I had been through. I was filled with joy because of the glorious and beautiful memories of everything I experienced with the Lord. I am so grateful to my Lord Jesus for that journey.

Within a few days, I was released and at last was able to be reunited with my four cherished children: Diana, Mikey, Mary, and Bernadette. I thought about the pleasure I felt being surrounded with so much love and peace. We laughed together, and I poured out my love on them! I would often cry aloud with a big smile on my face, "Thank you, Lord, for bringing me back home! Thank you, Jesus!" I knew it was by the grace of God that I was given a chance at life on Earth again, and I was overjoyed to be reunited with my children.[36]

Since I became a Christian in 1986, my life has been completely dedicated to serving God. A lot of my spiritual growth has taken place in Jacksonville, Florida, thanks to Dr. Bonzon and his wife, Tita. My heart is eternally grateful for this couple's commitment in supporting me and my family, mentoring me, and overseeing my spiritual

---

35 1 Corinthians 2:9-10 (NKJV): But as it is written: "Eye has not seen, nor ear heard, nor have entered into the heart of man the things which God has prepared for those who love Him." But God has revealed them to us through His Spirit. For the Spirit searches all things, yes, the deep things of God.

36 Romans 8:18-19 (NKJV): For I consider that the sufferings of this present time are not worthy to be compared with the glory which shall be revealed in us. For the earnest expectation of the creation eagerly waits for the revealing of the sons of God.

development by persistently taking me to church services and Bible studies where I was able to learn about and mature in my relationship with God.

Shortly after I came back to live in Jacksonville for a second time in 1994, I returned to New Life Christian Fellowship—my current church, which I began attending in 1986. During this time period, I got involved in the children's ministry for eleven years. I went on to welcome foster children into my home: an infant girl, who was just two weeks old, and her brother, who was born thirteen months later. I got to pick him up at the Beaches Hospital and took very good care of those two infants as if they were my own. At the time of writing this, they are now sixteen and fifteen years old. I am still involved in their lives by occasionally providing for their personal needs and consistently showing them God's love. I have also assisted eight destitute single mothers get back on their feet. This has been a large part of my ministry, and I am honored to do the Lord's work in this way.

While I was serving the Lord by helping little children that needed God's love, my husband was not very supportive. He was not happy with me being a Christian. He liked his worldly life, which was eventually the cause of our divorce. No matter what we sacrifice for the Lord, it is always worth it just to be close to Him. I am fully committed to serving the Lord with my whole life.

Back in 2014, I was led to establish an outreach ministry to the homeless in Jacksonville, Florida and have been serving my community in this way ever since. I thank

Jesus for the people He has brought alongside me. Our group has been hand-picked by God to do the work of His Kingdom by serving the poor.

For example, I met Neil and Neolla Hanekom, who are members of my church, in 2017 through a sequence of supernatural events. They were sent to me by God and came at a critical time in my life when I needed their support, while many others chose to overlook me because they were too busy and unavailable. Neil and Neolla have become an essential part of our outreach ministry and have partnered with me in many significant ways. We have been serving the homeless together since 2018, along with the rest of our amazing team: my son Mikey, my daughter Mary, and my friends Debbie, Mary Anne, Barbara, Janice, Don and Myrna, and Barb—and everyone else who has served with us in the past. Since accepting the Lord as my Savior, I have spent my life serving and winning souls for our Lord Jesus Christ and will continue to do so until He calls me home!

I have felt compelled to share my story for many years and have done so on a smaller scale than this; however, in this season of my life I have sensed a gentle push from God to release my testimony to the world. I know God allowed me to have that divine experience because His love for humanity is boundless. He longs for everyone to come to the knowledge of Christ and spend eternity in Heaven. I am merely a vessel whom He chose to reveal the reality of Heaven here on Earth. I am very honored to do my part in sharing His message with you, which is that of His endless love, His salvation, and His soon return. Please do not take this lightly and consider whether you are on the right path. The Bible says in Matthew 7:13-14 (NKJV) that "wide is the gate and broad is the way that leads to destruction, and there are many who go in by it. Because narrow is the gate and difficult is the way which leads to life, and there are few who find it." Be the one who finds the narrow path—the only one that leads to eternity in Heaven!

READER'S REFLECTIONS
(by AMBER PEÑA)

The book of John says that Jesus is the Word of God who came to live as a man in your place. It says He lived a perfect life in your place and died on the cross in order to pay the punishment for your sin. He has made a way to this narrow path that makes you free and saved from sin!

1. *Turn your focus to His sacrifice for you, thank Him, and give Him your whole life to Him as a response.*

2. *Express all you are willing to give up as you worship Him for all He has done for your eternal salvation. Hold nothing back. He will give you the "want to" and the strength. He's worth it all. Write it to Him, say it aloud, or sing it to Him.*

_____

_____

_____

_____

_____

_____

_____

_____

_____

_____

_____

*Every thought that comes from Jesus will be confirmed through His written Word, so you can always use the Bible later to confirm His voice to your heart.

"Epilogue"

BY BARBARA GIBSON

There was a war in Heaven. The war was between two angels—Lucifer and Michael. Lucifer rebelled against everything in Heaven. He was a liar and an accuser of the saints, and his goal was to rule in place of God. Lucifer and his army, along with Michael and his army, fought. Michael and his army prevailed, and Lucifer and his followers were thrown (like lightening) to Earth and the seas.

Since the fall of man—that is, Adam and Eve, whom God created on Earth, failed to resist Lucifer's (now called Satan) temptation by disobeying the almighty God's orders and eating from the tree of good and evil (as stated in Genesis, the first book of the Bible)—sin entered into the world, and with sin came the curse of death. So, from the day we are born, our physical bodies are aging, deteriorating, and will eventually die. That was not God's original plan. In His love for us, He granted us free will. He set down rules for us to live by and to guide us along so that we would not stumble or fall. God is a gentleman and will never force us to love Him or live for Him.

At some point, God became sad and was sorry that He created man. He wanted to destroy all of mankind, including the animals on the Earth, birds in the air, and fish in the sea. He would have if it were not for grace!

Only by His love and grace are we saved! To do this required a sacrifice—and not just a small sacrifice—a sacrifice of death, in order to reverse the original curse. So, the incarnate God (known as the second part of the triune (trinity) God, came down from Heaven, was born of a woman, lived a sinless life on Earth for thirty-three years. He died a merciless death on a cross as a sacrifice to pay for the sins of man which can never be paid by good works or obeying any laws.

> *But to all who did receive Him, to those who believed in His name, He gave the right to become children of God—children born not of blood, nor of the desire or will of man, but born of God....*
>
> **John 1:12-13 (BSB)**

Dear Reader,

There are many, many accounts of testimonies, similar to our author, Bella Lamm, from others who were taken up to Heaven. Bella's testimony is particularly unusual. The entire time Bella was in Heaven, she was still considered alive on Earth, and she understood that she was alive because at times she acted out her old human nature of fear, jealousy, anxiousness—even while walking with Jesus.

Bella did not just "find" herself in Heaven; Jesus extended His hand beckoning her to come with Him. Bella knew about Jesus but had not yet accepted Him as the Savior from her sins. That did not stop Jesus from loving her, inviting her to His Heaven, and even showing her places that many others have not seen. He did not judge her for her behavior when she was there. He did not even judge her for her lack of knowledge and belief in Him at the time. Also, while there, Jesus showed her Hell. She recognized many famous people, including a very nice woman she had grown up with. She witnessed all of them being tortured, begging for relief, and calling out to anyone who would listen; however, when Bella questioned Jesus, He said, "It is too late for them." All of the souls in Hell were given an opportunity to come to Jesus during their life on Earth, but they rejected Him.

Beloved, Bella's prayer for you is for now. Her hope is that after reading this book, you will come to the knowledge of what you must do to be saved, what you must do to have your sins forgiven, what you must do to secure your destiny—to know that when you die, you are assured that you will go to Heaven to be with Jesus and spend eternity with Him. It is not a coincidence that you picked up this book—or that you were even given this book. You were chosen by God for this day and time. In His love, He is calling you, beckoning you to come and accept Him as your Lord and Savior.

For our citizenship is in heaven, from which we also eagerly wait for the Savior, the Lord Jesus Christ, 21 who will transform our lowly body that it may be conformed to His glorious body, according to the working by which He is able even to subdue all things to Himself.

(Philippians 3:20-21 NKJV)

If you are ready and willing, there is a sample prayer below just for you. This will change your life forever!

Lord Jesus, for too long I've kept you out of my life. I know that I am a sinner and that I cannot save myself. No longer will I close the door when I hear you knocking. By faith, I gratefully receive your gift of salvation. I am ready to trust you as my Lord and Savior. Thank you, Lord Jesus, for coming to Earth. I believe you are the Son of God who died on the cross for my sins and rose from the dead on the third day. Thank you for bearing my sins and giving me the gift of eternal life. I believe your words are true. Come into my heart, Lord Jesus, and be my Savior. Amen.

9 798887 380957